LEVERAGE

LEVERAGE

JONATHAN HOLDEN

University Press of Virginia
Charlottesville

for my children

ALANNA *and* ZACHARY

THE UNIVERSITY PRESS OF VIRGINIA
Copyright © 1983 by the Rector and Visitors
of the University of Virginia

First published 1983

Library of Congress Cataloging in Publication Data

Holden, Jonathan.
    Leverage.
    I. Title.
PS3558.034775L4   1983   811'.54   83-14744
ISBN 0-8139-1011-0

Printed in the United States of America

Foreword

"Oh Lord! don't invite *her*; she'll do nothing but talk about her
children all evening!" But we do and she does and it's dreadful.
It's not that families are dull; what's more dangerous, more
demanding? It's that some people have nothing to say, while
certain others who do, won't. That may be sound policy—someone
could be listening. And any human group (like any human
belief) survives only by our mute and mutual agreement not to
see too much—especially not the key facts of the arrangement.
It's true that the group is less obviously needed than it once was.
Yet, like it or not, and try to chisel on our commitment as we
all do, our need for the group, the family, remains. Finally, of course,
some people will bore you even when they *have* something they
want to say—will put you to sleep telling you the name and
qualities of your next lover, the time and circumstances of your
death, the corner where you lost the golden apple.

Anyway, go ahead and invite Jonathan Holden. He'll talk
about his family so that your ears, your brain, your feelings will
tingle for days. He *has* something to say; he says it with force and
grace. (What in the world is he doing in poetry *these* days?)
His voice has some of that energy he found as a boy with a friend's
toy train transformer and a pie plate of saltwater:

> [we] *drank through our fingers*
> *the current's purr,*
> *dialing that bird-heartbeat*
> *higher, riding its flutter until*
> *both hands were bucked*
> *out of water.*

Holden offers us the ordinary, the commonplace, the "redundant,"
but with the juice flipped on—brings us the jolt of the diurnal,
switched on; the shock of the normal, plugged in. Most poets
who try to cut us in to our own circuits, blow the fuses; he connects
things so rightly that we glow and illuminate ourselves.

Holden's titles, alone, suggest his concern with "how much /
slow work it takes to build the familiar":

Home from Work
Family Busk
The Swimming Pool
Cutting Beetle-blighted Ponderosa Pine
Washing My Son
Making Things Grow
Nesting
Sunday Breakfast
Catch with My Son
With Father, Cleaning Out the Spring
Cleaning the Flue
Fixing the Deep-well Jet Pump

If he (or his poems' speaker) picks up his son after work, he is
suddenly back in his own childhood sniffing over his father for
the day's news; if he bathes the boy, he himself becomes a child
painting a model plane. In the delightful "Making Things Grow"
he cultivates the garden just as he must his family, providing
a patient sprinkling of affection:

what all unkissed places everywhere
expect, the tongue expects, what this
lonely place on the neck expects and
what, on tiptoe, this place on the
throat expects and what this
neglected place expects. And this place
here. And here.

Against the controlled shock of the train transformer, the
the alternating current of family life, we also see our vulnerability
to the total shock of physical nature, to the uncontrolled energies
of our own rages and passions; our internal nature. Again and
again we see the wind breaking loose into storm, the total
shapeless sky rushing in at us, the lightning splitting our own nest,

our own brain, like a geode. We are no doubt threatened even by the imagined "voltage" inside Mary Devore's sweater! Against that fiercer nature, our best constructions are frail, our best reasonings "hardly any help at all." In "The Third Party" we listen to a brilliant and successful woman scientist—"But as she analyzed her rotten marriage / she was plain stupid"—and eventually learn that

> the speech of grief,
> a dead end in itself,
> so satisfying, so useless,
> is the same tautology, the last
> cliché, the one area of expertise
> in which, sooner or later,
> we get as good as anybody.

Holden shows, also, how this local everyday life of ours expands into our wider social concerns: "Why We Bombed Haiphong" and "Politics." In a specially delightful group of poems, it spreads further into our conception of religion: "Hell" turns out to be an eternal high school Drivers' Ed. class; "God" turns out to be our dentist; election to the blessed turns out to be a "Shoe Store" and the "annointed" feet of one's own children.

Perhaps we do not see all we might (should we ask for everything at once?) of the horrors of the family, the dangers in its necessary limitations. We do, however, find hints in "Peter Rabbit" where the commandment "Don't!" becomes a kind of sun, a source of light and energy that gives the world its shadows. Only through disobedience does Peter come to know he *is* alive. The same impulsion operates in the poems about the boyhood gang and their disobediences, their destructiveness, their rage that "the world is coming to an end" which drives them to break all the glass in the city dump. Even though they end up feeling "satisfied,"

> The dump looked just the way
> it had before; we hadn't made a dent.
> Even then it was too late.

What the speaker learns, in a letter "To a Boyhood Friend . . ." is the deep importance of craft, of leverage. He must learn to control this energy not only into the skills that clean his flue, build his father's swimming pool, cook his children's breakfast, but especially to transform that rage, that drive into his art. Sometimes I worry that Holden is almost too successful, has almost too much craft, that his poems *do* say just and only what he means. Yet I also suspect that much of the time—without, I hope, his conscious devising—they are really about the way he writes a poem. That is nowhere more charmingly suggested than in "Fixing the Deep-well Jet Pump" with its initial fumbling and laboring in the slimy dark, its delight in coming up with the right name for things

> *With a dollop of gray*
> *axle grease I buttered*
> *the sealer, forced it*
> *down over the main bearing,*
> *then one by one restrung*
> *the drive shaft*
> *with its deep-sea shells*

and its triumphant ending:

> *We flipped on the juice.*
> *The jet tensed, the water*
> *firmed, came surging through*
> *the pump, and the evening*
> *was watertight.*

Though that last image will only be clear and fully appropriate once you've read the whole poem, this does suggest, and quite rightly, the kind of craftsman's skill Holden has. It's the exploratory drive one sees, now and then, in repairmen, mechanics, farmers— the delight in doing something just to find out how the damn thing works.

W. D. SNODGRASS

Acknowledgments

The author and publisher wish to thank the following magazines for permission to reprint certain poems.

The Aspen Anthology, for "The '50 Storm," by permission of Aspen Leaves, Inc.

The Black Warrior Review, for "Shoe Store."

The Chariton Review, for "To a Boyhood Friend: How We Changed."

Chelsea, for "Politics."

CutBank, for "Family Busk," by permission of the editors.

The Georgia Review, for "Cutting Beetle-blighted Ponderosa Pine."

The Iowa Review, for "Peter Rabbit."

The Kansas Quarterly, Vol. 12.1 (Winter 1980), for "God" and "Washing My Son."

The Midwest Quarterly, for "Fixing the Deep-well Jet Pump," "Nesting," and "The Sorrow of Captain Hook," by permission of the editor-in-chief.

The Missouri Review, for "An American Boyhood."

Modern Poetry Studies, for "Cleaning the Flue," copyright © 1980. By permission.

New Letters, for "Why We Bombed Haiphong," by permission.

The New Mexico Humanities Review, for "Hell," by permission of the editors.

The Northwest Review, for "At the Airport."

The Ohio Review, for "Home from Work."

Open Places, for "Making Things Grow," by permission of the editor.

Poet and Critic 9:2, for "Leverage," by permission of the editor.

Poet Lore, for "Visiting Agnes," by permission.

Poetry, for "Fire," "How to Throw Apples," "One-ring Circus," "Salvation," and "The Third Party."

Poetry Now, for "Glass" and "The Swimming Pool," by permission.

Quarterly West, for "Seventeen," by permission of the editor.

The Sonora Review, for "Births," "Catch with My Son," and "Sunday Breakfast," by permission of the editor.

The Western Humanities Review, for *"Toilers of the Sea*: Albert Pinkham Ryder," copyright © 1979. By permission.

The Wisconsin Review, for "With Father, Cleaning Out the Spring."

The author wishes to thank the National Endowment for the Arts for its generous support.

Contents

I. The Sorrow of Captain Hook

II. Salvation

III. Leverage

I

THE SORROW OF
CAPTAIN HOOK

THE SORROW OF
CAPTAIN COOK

An American Boyhood

There was little important
to do but chew gum, or count
the ways a flipped jackknife
caught in the dirt.
One Sunday afternoon I had an idea.
We clamped the cables of Tommy
Emory's train transformer
to a steel pie plate
filled with saltwater
and drank through our fingers
the current's purr,
dialing that bird-heartbeat
higher, riding its flutter until
both hands were bucked
out of water.
                We knew
we were wasting our time,
though we had nothing
but time. Our parents
moved vague among their great
worries, remote
as the imperatives of weather.
And the stars appeared on schedule
to run their dim, high errands
again, leaving us lost
in the long boredom of our childhood,
flipping our knives in the dust,
waiting to find out just how
in this world we were going
to be necessary.

The Sorrow of Captain Hook

They think the crocodile is a big joke
that crawled out of some comic book and winked.
They think they can bathe in the lagoon's
blue curls without even getting wet. But Hook
knows better. He can fully appreciate the tick,
tick, tick. He knows that the crooked fault
of the crocodile's grin is not a smile at all.
It might as well be a crack in the rock,
the edge of a landscape closing involuntarily
against the windy sky. He knows that
the crocodile's appetite doesn't discriminate;
the gleam in its eye is just an accident
of light on a shiny bolt. Even here on dry land
he is not safe. For the reptile swims
in anything, in the dirt, in the light, in
the supple trunks of the coconut trees.
As the mild afternoon declines
it slides toward you in every shadow, subtly,
without crinkling a single twig, without
breathing. Hook has a secret.
There's no clock at work in the crocodile's gut.
The vague tack-hammer progress of the tock
is all in his mind. Hook would warn
Peter Pan if he could. But Pan won't trust him;
he's too busy rescuing Tiger Lily, setting up
ambushes, laying plans. Wendy is peacefully
sewing his shadow back on. The six lost boys
are still sleeping it off. The morning
sunlight is pure. It is exactly room temperature.
Except for the faint zing of Tinkerbell
in the warm coconut grove, there isn't
a ripple of air. Each rock, each magnified

bit of sand, the serrated edge of every
emerald frond is stuck in the perfect light.
Beyond, the sea naps in the sun
and the Jolly Roger sits, its toy sails idle.
Poor Hook stares out over Never-Never Land alone,
the only adult in the world.

Visiting Agnes

By then, whatever that difficult name
was, making itself at home
in her nervous system,
had disconnected it, had all
but assumed her name, had stripped
her of her right
to communicate with her own
tongue, her right to swallow
food, her right to eat,
of the dignity to even
hold her spit, twisted
her into this small,
curiously wrought practical joke
whose eyes would squirt
this way and that, yet which
contained, still, some last seed
of Agnes, whose wheezing,
the doctor said, was laughter
at the crack I'd made about
our friend Dot's henpecking poor Pete,
part of my loud pep talk as I sat
there like some young attorney
encouraging a client, mouthing the pat
articles of law, swallowing
for the luxury of it.

Home from Work

I lift my son, let him
sniff me closely as I
used to sniff the sweat
off Father's bristling tweed
jacket every night.

His hug was redolent of miles.
Glints of mica from sidewalk
grit hovered in the wool
with other people's breath,
spent shaving lotion
like a stale cocktail
and the brine of fish.

That bitter wool had picked
up everything: peppermint
stuck to it, and blue
exhaust, hairs, handshakes,
fingernail clippings,
little shells, a little
powder from the moon.

I clung, sniffing, searching
his pockets for where
he'd come from.
The wool burned.

At the Airport

My father's profile makes a stiff, bright beak
that keeps peering forward, myopically intent.
He's like a puzzled owl because he doesn't
see very well, a puzzled hawk. He hobbles
into the metal detector without a peep.
Wryly, my mother follows him. Together
they resemble two fine pieces of oak furniture
that match, seasoned hardwood which if you hit
too fat a nail in it would split; it's all
ridiculous. But they're too tired
to protest. With this four-hour operation
ahead of them above the earth, home's
their only interest.
The guards frisk Father with a brisk,
surgical distaste. Somehow they know
that if there's anything ticking underneath
his coat, it won't blow up; it will run down
quietly with a little cough; they let him go.
Watching it, I want to yell: You're wasting
your time! Can't you tell there's no
metal in them anymore? They're just old folks,
all wood! Can't you even trust fine oak?
But I shuffle in behind them with the rest,
submit in silence, then at the gate
hold them against my chest, carefully hug
both these bunches of dry briars. It hurts.
We huddle there, our last conspiracy.
We don't dare speak. We'd be discovered.
The little danger left in us would burst.

Family Busk

I wish this stuff would catch
and cuss us out the way it used to
when we ripped up the blackberry
patch. It's too wet. The hay
on top is caked, half compost clogged
with steam, the smoke inside like
thick, curdled milk.

I wish these were the tangled
bedsprings of those briars we used
to burn; they coiled like whips,
their thorns the size of thumbnails;
when they clung, they could tear
a sweater up into loose string.

That stuff piled up almost too
fast for us—a dried rage.
When we lit the fuse on it, we had
to circle it with rakes, beat away
its heat, sneak in under to scuff out
the skirmishes it set. And there

it goes, all the times I banged
upstairs behind my brother, flung
him on his bed where he contracted,
shrank his head like a turtle inside
the pillows, bared his arm; the years
I farmed a purple garden on it
with my fist. There go all

the bitter silences my father
kept behind closed doors, trying
to work; the times my mother valiantly
explained what made him tick. There
goes the core—that one, malicious,
carrot-colored tongue, lolling
out of control above our heads—it
spoke for us, it simplified everything
again.

More smoke blooms up, this warm
mist, it almost smothers us. My mother
bravely shovels some wet leaves, working
around the edges with the same deft
patience that she cooks a duck.
This stuff won't burn, and, still,
she won't let go of that stupid
rake she doesn't need.

The Swimming Pool

Long after he'd wearied of the work
I recall my father sloshing in hip boots,
ignoring the mosquitoes on his back
to lay by hand, around the stone
swimming pool he'd built, this tile
drain to divert the brook when it
turned brown in thunderstorms, how
he grunted as he pried up each sucking
shovelful of muck, his face
a shiny little mask of wrinkled sweat,
hating every minute of it.
And I remember how, later, in July,
when the wet heat would make you
claustrophobic and despair
he'd step up to that pool—
shy almost—gingerly dip in a toe,
exclaim wryly, then begin the ritual,
first rinse the arms,
then wash the chest,
his legs meanwhile feeling their way
on tiptoe as he waded forward, becoming
shorter and shorter, the cold lip
of the water crawling up his stomach
until, ready to receive the cold,
he'd lie back on his back and sigh,
then close his eyes as though
that pool could never give him back
enough or fast enough or long enough
all that he'd put into it.

Cutting Beetle-blighted Ponderosa Pine

In one week we dismantled
the little old country of the sky—
that wonderful colored
map. At anchor in its blue
harbors, between civilizations,
the big clouds would ride.
With my chain saw I opened
tracts of raw sky, cleared
until the last land in sight,
our single pier, our outpost
was one grandfather
of a tree. I chipped at
its trunk, chipped,
scaling bark-scabs off until
the hatchet skimmed wet
meat. But there were
those bluish-gray streaks
in it. I kept the saw shaking
and digging until I struck
the nerve. The tree
shivered, its spine groaning
in its throat.
When it let out a deep
croak and, shuddering,
sank into the dust, the rest
of the sky—nothing
to hold it back, sky without
a profile—rolled over
my head, more sky than anyone
can handle.

The '50 Storm

I lay for some time in that gray room
and concentrated. Yes, the house was
definitely moving. We were adrift.
Surf roared in the sycamore.
A voice wheedled around the gutter.
A second reedy voice joined.
They flirted by the southeast window,
raced away, fled back, singing
higher, clinging to the corner
of the house so violently that the floor
quivered, the storm windows buzzed,
the ark shuddered uncontrollably
as the sea climbed the east side,
then slowly heavily receded
and the two voices came spinning back,
nagging and jeering, shriller
and meaner around the gutter
and every seam in the ark strained.

Barefoot downstairs into the darkened
hall I snuck, the first one awake.
Our house was busy, every corner
at work. The kitchen creaked.
Wherever the sea rammed it
the wall talked back. From out front
I could hear hysteria in the hundred-
foot Norway spruce. The back door was
yanked from my hand, wind blew
the breath from my mouth, half bullied me
off the porch, driving sparse shots
of rain horizontally like bees. I held
my own. The air was lightheaded, too

warm. We were far from shore. Sticks,
spars, shingles and strange shells
had washed up on the lawn. The sea swarmed
low over the chimney where the black
peak of the spruce gnashed back
and forth denying everything.

Breakfast was pathetic.
We fidgeted before our orange juice
and eggs while the house did the talking.
Mother was drying dishes when the power
sank. Now there was nothing left
to do except to sit,
to concentrate on that stampede.
Finally in such storms you drop everything.
You tighten up, almost eager
for the worst, and patrol the windows.
You become an ironist.
If you're alert, perhaps you'll get
a snapshot of the End.
But the End is fickle. Nearly noon
when I realized that the east was wrong.
The Pardees' spruce grove was lopsided;
its profile had gone crazy,
half its teeth knocked out.

Each time I looked a new excavation glared
until that countenance was a vacant snarl,
unrecognizable. We redoubled our patrol—
from the sycamore to the spruce and back.
The east was spoiled.
We had to save the north, the south.
While we watched, they wouldn't dare fall.
A shadow passed the bathroom window
and the front yard was buried under spruce

thrashing around in its last throes.
The sky, no longer tethered to that tree,
blasted us. It was totally expressionless.
And I remember yelling in its face
as it grabbed at my voice, yelling
because this day was so unfair
as if I'd known then how much
slow work it takes to build the familiar,
how much of my own work was blown away.

Fate

I could picture it as a jagged edge.
Each time our month-old son
made another lunge to breathe
it tripped him up, his breath
would catch, stagger into coughs.
I guess we were possessive, we thought
that by themselves our arms ought
to be enough to insulate him. Stubborn,
I'd stamp outdoors into the snow for wood.
It was ten below, the air a bramble patch.
I resented it, I wanted to trample
its stalks, crush it underfoot.
But it was too green to break.
It merely bent, sprang back behind me,
stung again. The toughened snow
winced beneath my boots.
Finally, to mute that edge,
we fortified him by the humidifier.
That didn't work. White mold flourished
on the windows, new shoots slipped
through the cracks. I'd whet the fire.
But the minute we rested
in the clearing it cut
its blades would rust, we could feel
the silence outside growing fat.

There is a common little word. Fate.
I hadn't cared before what it meant.
It's not a euphemism, it means
that anger is a pathetic religion,
almost a faith. And that we're ignorant.
When at last we relented, left him

with his apricot-colored haze of hair
packaged in the cellophane wrapper
of the oxygen tent,
I knew we'd relinquished him to Fate.
That night, alone, as never before
I could appreciate how indifferently
moonlight always did assail the snow.
Sometimes we're too late to feel.
The facts we face are odds.
Totally exposed, you simply wait, calm,
as I did at the window, fascinated
with some funny twist of matter,
watching a cloud adjacent to the moon,
eccentric, wrinkled like my palm,
watching its edge drift, find its direction:
grief. Or faith, that other accident.

Washing My Son

Zack's eyes can't
focus, but his skin
can. He squirms
as I hone him down,
tickle his feet, lather
up his neck, erase
these foamy four-lane
highways down his back
and wash around
his thimble-size wet
cock. He wants to be
touched all over,
rubbed behind his ears
like this, his neck
stroked, even
his navel's little map
explored. Scrubbing
him is polishing
this whittled spear
of wood until
that new wood shines
and he's firm,
sanded down all
over with my hands,
healed up
like a model airplane
you just made over
into silver. I kiss
him again. All
the decals go on
perfectly.

Toilers of the Sea: Albert Pinkham Ryder

A brisk wind was crisping the edges of the ground swell
white when after breakfast the three of them set sail.
It was the kind of morning which the Chamber
of Commerce would have advertised, the weather
marching along right-handed and loud, a bright
brass band out of the west, bugles and trombones
hitting flats and sharps off the cold water's faces.
They were going to have their picnic of peanut
butter and jelly sandwiches on the water and be home
shortly after lunch. What happened that day we can only
guess. Perhaps an odd pallor in the sun was the first
sign, a left-handed hint in the light the start
of the climate's total eclipse. Perhaps it was when
they noticed that suddenly all the gulls were
gone, that the ocean was noiseless; for the sea
here is luxurious, it has many slippery laws of its own.
And when they realized that they could no longer hear
each other talk, what must have gone through their minds?
The sky was gloved by then. A warm wind was swelling
their solitary sail, but they couldn't tell where
it was coming from, there are no stars here.
There is no land in sight. All they could have seen
when they looked for the sun was this fat lusterless star
which will not set. The pull of that new pole on the boat
was otherworldly. Their compass was conked.
Nothing would work. All their watches must have stopped
together, a hundred years ago, leaving these three
silhouettes sitting perfectly still in the negative
of that airy Chamber of Commerce morning,
letting their black boat run wild before the wind
seeking a passage back.

Making Things Grow

All day we've had to haul around
and readjust the garden hose's coils
to keep the mouths in that thin soil
kissed evenly. They must be loose,
unpuckered. I want them ready
to receive the sun, and wildly,
the way our daughter wrings milk out
when she makes her bottle chirp
or drinks up sleep, her paws curled
as if clutching out at it; the way
she digests the yawn that widens
through her arms each time she hoists
herself upright with her hands, or laps
up what it is she studies in my eyes.
That's what the garden, though it won't
wake me up at night, expects of me;
what all unkissed places everywhere
expect, the tongue expects, what this
lonely place on the neck expects and
what, on tiptoe, this place on the
throat expects and what this
neglected place expects. And this place
here. And here.

II

SALVATION

Salvation

You can always recognize the saved.
They smell of soap. A serene half-smile
is welded on their faces, their eyes
wet with that stratospheric light
that makes the white anvils at the peaks
of thunderheads in the late afternoon heat
almost holy. The New Vernon Presbyterian
Church Choir assumed that expression
as it rose to sing—old Mrs. Greer,
Tommy Emory and Penny May who'd take
the bus to school with me on weekdays.
The hair on the back of my neck froze
as the starch-robed ranks of that community
stiffened up to sing, their eyes moist,
fixed upward in the rush of certainty.
You could almost envy them.

For suddenly everything was black and white
as a Rubens painting of the Apocalypse:
so high above you have to crane your neck
is a country club in peaks of morning snow.
Poised in that stadium of stone and cloud
the banks of the saved gaze straight ahead
and sing, a hillside of white wheat
writhing in the wind. At first you think
they're wooing you to join—until you notice
what's going on below, see what they're doing.

Those green thrones of daisies where the saved
recline slip off into a gray rock face,
a granite gorge, the lower ledges half
obscured by fumes seeping up from an open
sewer bubbling at the base. The lake's alive
with bodies, some human, the rest reptile.
Horned demons with forked tongues, fetid
steam jetting out of their ears, are going
to work on the front row. One is goosing
a floundering woman whose tongue protrudes.
Another is taking, with shark's teeth,
a chunk from her thigh. Later they're going
to enjoy some activities too gross to mention.
They're in no hurry, they have plenty of time.

A man whose eyes bug can't work his thighs
from between two burning sides of beef.
There's mounting panic to get out.
It's a mob, a fountain of postures threshing
upward, clutching at the cliff's thin ledges,
fingers slipping. Bodies, buttocks dripping
slime, hang by their nails halfway up the rock
face, trembling to climb straight into the clouds
that seem so low. A few have made it.
Still out of breath, no sooner do they haul
themselves up on the lawn, they whirl
around. They're happy now. They wear
the same peaceful vague smile the singers have.
Some pick up staffs and wield them like long
gaffs to gouge at the eyes of the sinners.
Body after body is pried loose, sent kicking
through the air all the way back down
to the bottom of the cliff where they float
prone, blowing bubbles in the muck
and no longer seem to care.

Above, the clouds' frilled edges shine,
the petals of some phosphorescent flower
carved against the bitter stratosphere.
The music swells. Each aria's whetted,
a fine instrument of pain. Inside her
the soprano keeps a silver sword
which she sends out to hurt all sinners.
Every obscenity I know I'd scream at her—
at all those pink faces scrubbed behind the ears—
but their anthem is so loud they couldn't hear.
The bass triumphantly tramps on in brazen boots
leaving bleeding tracks along the slumped
backs bobbing in the lake. The saved can't hear.
They don't know what the hell they're doing.
Nothing could enter their sweet minds so long as
they keep up their beautiful, idiotic singing.

Hell

You will wake up
in your old seat
behind Pete Bowerbank
in 8th-period Driver
Ed. Tommy Conger will
be there too, in back of
you, squelching his
Wrigley's, breathing
spearmint down your neck.
And Lyle Smith,
who had the loudest
artificial burp—
bulked against the side
board, honking
snores. Your desk
will be the same scarred
tablet, prehistoric,
with the purple fossils
in it—the blue rune
that said *Eat the
Root,* the one that read
Bird Bites. Chuck
Spino will have his comb
out to lubricate his hair.
It will be May,
and as you wait
in the lighted cave
of Room 101—wait to
evolve while Mr. McIntyre
repeats Leave four
car-lengths at forty
miles an hour—

you will think and
think of the little wet
click Mary Devore's
lips make as she smiles,
imagine the voltage
in her sweater, try
to think how
outdoors on the tight
green diamond
the throw from third
to first is easy—a lilt,
a flicker, bull's-eye.
And McIntyre will go on,
and the lukewarm New Jersey
haze, like a light
perfume, will stretch
south, almost to the bridge,
to Bayonne.

Seventeen

That June before the judge gave
Rennie Dodd his choice—jail or joining
the Marines—we were already on patrol, part
of the nervous prod of traffic
along the cement tundra called U.S. 46,
observing protocol. Drunk,
swerving at oncoming cars, giving
pedestrians the finger,
we'd rake the AM tuner's roar
for bursts of action at the front, chasing
that low blaze on the horizon.
But this was 1959. There was no war.
We were invited
nowhere. We had to cross the state line
to buy beer. Our tires peeling their awkward
falsetto, we'd head out on a mission, sure
that, this time, the skyline was inviting
us, and eager to go, ready
to be recruited by the night.

God

It is to this stolid
inexpressive man
who washes his soft
hands religiously in
soap that you will close
your eyes, leave yourself
wide open and confess—
entrusting the warm
crannies of your mouth,
your tongue, the wet
secrets which only he
and your lovers notice.
With a long face
he will lean over you,
his pink fingers
probing for the weak
points you've neglected.
All your failings will show
up in your mouth,
magnified in the blunt
snouts of your teeth.
Emptied, you will stare
up at the placid
light, wondering if
it will hurt much.
An angel will appear
and set a tray before
you, a row of dainties
laid out neatly
on a napkin. Through closed
eyes you'll hear utensils
click. Each point will be

a moral. The drill
will chirrup, a stainless
steel canary, an abstract
pang; he'll spoon-
feed you with pain,
and as you dine on it
slowly you'll feel
yourself go pure.

Shoe Store

How foolish my own children both
seem as the salesman swirls
around them, lacing, pressing
with thumbs a stiff toe, touching
them lightly, flattering,
How does that feel?
They answer with passive smiles.
Now, gingerly, on that carpeted
altar, their feet annointed,
they learn to walk again.
They strut and turn and strut
as if their feet were torches
shedding glamor. They are far
away, they've forgotten already
who they are. The shoes
have won them. The salesman
laces them up and leads
them to the mirrors.

One-ring Circus

Something of hemp there might
have been, of sawdust, pulleys
in that swarthy woman, picaresque
in her wrestler's shoulders.
Something of tendons, of pain
in the taste of the drooling
tooth-pocked rubber bit she took
in her teeth to hang by her neck, twirling
midair, head yanked all
the way back.
When the baby elephant—tusks
hacksawed off for the tentative safety
of cash—was ushered out,
a moral might have been in the hook
at the tip of the gentleman's cane
the ringmaster like a conductor
used to collect the slack
clay folds of the animal up
onto the stool,
a moral on which even the elephant,
its eye a knot in rock,
concentrated with philosophical calm.
The April sun stained the patched sails
of the big top. Over
the din of the generator
an electric organ maintained the fanfare.
You might have smelt elegy there—
the idea of a brass band, tubas
harrumphing, spitting the sunlight, nodding
yes up Main Street on Saturday morning,
new paint on the wagons,
their fool's-gold gingerbread cornices

polished, the horses' sides
flush with the June sheen of meadows,
the lions dragging the rasps in their throats—
a parade as startling, brave
as the tulips. None of this
could happen.
Though the clown in the baggy pants
was too drunk to be sad,
and the juggler could never quite find
all the red balls at once,
this was not even the Circus of Failures.
It was no more than the world, no more
than the sum of its parts.

The Third Party

Her mind
was so much more than she—
it was a third party.
Like some large instrument
at the love-bed,
it made an exotic guest: able
to decide on its own
whether or not to participate.

Hurt people bear with them
a slightly puzzled look,
a scar between the eyes
where their grief is lodged,
a lead plummet.
I'd seen her, a scientist, delve
into a differential
equation like a boy rudely
unlocking an orange by
forcing the seams from the lobes
to spring it open.
But as she analyzed her rotten marriage
she was plain stupid.

There is no one, I think,
whose private life isn't more
or less unlovely than daily weather.
It's the country where our friends
all speak the same tongue.
Whatever you do,
every angle of the bones,
has been tried before.
And the speech of grief,

a dead end in itself,
so satisfying, so useless,
is the same tautology, the last
cliché, the one area of expertise
in which, sooner or later,
we get as good as anybody.

As she talked, her hand on mine,
heavy, opaque, and sad,
her heartbeat a mute syllable
typed out in code,
her beautiful mind—so
much better than she—could no more
save her than the pure
scaffolding of chamber music
as it goes up
can save the four, short
scholarly men huddled under it,
a quartet of carpenters
with too much on their hands,
measuring, filing, conferring
like mad to assemble
another section of an intelligence
almost too plausible.

Like a calculated smile, it,
too, might break
a man's heart or save
his life,
but is, indeed, heartless,
better than we are,
hardly any help at all.

Peter Rabbit

The sunlight was dull, it might have been
morning or evening before the word *Don't*
was said. The grass, if there were grass, might
have been gray, it didn't make any difference.
The temperature of the air outside the burrow
was normal. *Don't.* It cast all the shadows.
The sun shrank back into focus. He could see.
Under that harsh brilliant judgment
each whetted blade of grass had a black shadow.
And a gate was rearing against the sky,
a rebuke, a giant affront. He squeezed under it,
his heart twittering. Scritch. Scratch.
He could hear—a rake, a bee fizz as it rose
from a daisy, the wind's restless crowds
in the high reaches of the oak trees behind him,
wind encompassing fields for miles, birds
swinging on it, sparrow trapezes, wind,
enough sound to cover his tracks, *don't,*
don't, to make sly twitches, faint substitutions
of grass that could be other stealthy creatures,
decoys to draw the fire of Mr. McGregor,
as Peter, now sick with hunger, crept
toward the clenched hearts of the lettuce,
thinking, don't touch the hidden parts you've
heard about, don't finger the wet leaves, don't
spit them out. "Stop! Thief!" It sharpened
the shadows. *Don't. Don't.* The leaves poised.
Each wisp of darkness held out the cool
palm of its hand, its hollow of safety, a silk
suit to slip into, try on, cast off. He'd never
noticed such terrain. How its curves console,
its hills reveal. Without Mr. McGregor,

he might never have seen a pot before. "Stop! Thief!" The light was a nuisance. Each row was a bootstep. A scramble. A heartbeat. Each second a question. Each door a new answer. The gate was a daydream, and he was alive.

Why We Bombed Haiphong

When I bought bubble gum
to get new baseball cards
the B-52 was everywhere you looked.
In my high school yearbook
the B-52 was voted "Most Popular"
and "Most Likely to Succeed."

The B-52 would give you the finger
from hot cars. It laid rubber,
it spit, it went around in gangs,
it got its finger wet and sneered
about it. It beat the shit
out of fairies.

I remember it used to chase
Derek Remsen around at recess
every day. Caught, he'd scream
like a girl. Then the rest
of us pitched in and hit.

Politics

I guess it is only human to be
in this gray limbo by the window
watching the raucous birds outside
jockeying for position, eating
with deft decisive nods: yes, yes.
A male cardinal dips in, royalty,
scatters the sparrows, whips this
way and that, fiercely circumspect
in his black executioner's mask.
The sparrows, nervous snippets
of the shabby ground itself, change
places hurriedly, they're jittery.
But none questions its right to eat.
They're all political. They love
and hate power. Right now they eye
it resentfully but refuse to go away.
Stubborn, they shift around on the fringe
of the party while the big black-jacketed
starlings spit swearwords at each other,
snack, go for the eyes and snack
some more, a sleazy gang. It bursts
into the upper stories of the catalpa tree;
and the chickadees, quick, discreet,
always intent, checking the intruders
with sharp looks, circling, drop
a notch to the garage roof, down a notch
to the top of the fence, the last
notch down to the cold ground, the arena
where each is a full-time lobbyist
for the tiny wild industry that is itself.
Over and over they make the same
mean speech: we need energy. Gimmee this.

Mine. Get outatheway. Gimmee
this. This. With no more scruples
than either side of those big arguments
that make the weather roll
when the opposing elements are too loyal
and the carnage of the rain is incalculable.
It is only while we are human
that we waver like this by the window
and hang back, questioning our motives,
indulge the bitter luxury of hating ourselves,
our last chance to remain neutral
before, with the brown leaves of the sycamore
lying out there, we take sides.

III

LEVERAGE

Nesting

Before you move into a tree
learn the direction
of every crooked street.
Memorize the conventions
which sunlight adopts,
its poise on each twig,
its deft stride
and how, as it circles,
the whole precarious city
turns. That's how
you'll climb. By shortcuts.
By picking the footholds
which sunlight picks,
the imperceptible notches.
By trying perches
until your stance is so
solid, sunken in
the pitch of every crook
that even when the wind
loosens the seams
and bends the network
of your touch,
you keep your balance.
Any niche is your room.
To break it in, use it
hard, wear it in the rain,
working it down around
your skin until
the weather is rubbed
so well in the grain
that no cloud can nest
there without your help

and even storms will learn
some etiquette. Nail
on the walls the full
range of seasons.
And what you brought
impart, pack under every
loose board; work it into
each crack—a cache which
will shine like the brain
inside a geode
when the lightning splits
the tree apart.

Sunday Breakfast

This might just be the height
of luxury—to be sautéing
onions, your fingers steeped
in garlic, in hot
running water, in food
when outside the sunlight
glimpsed in the wires
seems scarcely a lick or
a promise or wardrobe enough
for the skinny branches
glinting, empty as coat hangers
that jostle each other.

You think how a grandfather, shadowing
his children's kids in the park,
might weigh on his features
the flimsy sun
like some faint ethereal song
he had long listened for,
once in his possession—
How, reminded by light, the faces
of the old still hearken
as if the landscape itself
remembered a kinder season,

maybe this one,
the sun trapped here on the rug
where the light seems tamed,
no harm left in it but warmth,
and your own children
who do not know what luxury
is, are picnicking,

playing a board game
as you go on opening cans,
connecting parts of the kitchen,
confirming yourself in the odor
of coffee and garlic,
making a breakfast as redundant
as you can.

Fire

This wolf-dog is
the best defense
against too big a dose
of silence
when the stringency
of your own blood in your head
could hem you in.
This walking hunger
will eat out of your hand.
It's half intelligent.

It would turn wild,
hunt anything, hunt me
down too if I didn't
keep it domesticated, fit
bones between its teeth,
let it hunt dead logs.
They can't escape.
It combs their sides
and wags its tail,
my dog with wolf in it,

and sniffs around the room,
teasing the corner of your eye,
noticing the walls, the ceiling,
fuller than the sound
of running water as it goes
on reading to you quietly
reciting this matter
which, even if it did
have words,
you wouldn't understand.

Catch with My Son

It's evening
out on the slovenly lawn
as he tries to connect us
with a straight line.
But the loose thing
has no sense of direction.
It gets snarled in the grass.
I hold it up again
in the soft remnants of sun
for him to see
and pull it taut,
take aim, hint
what I could do with it.
Draw a bead on the walnut tree.
Blow his head off cleanly.
I wind up again
slowly
like stroking a knife
on a whetstone, *silk*
silk, till the edge
of the edge is out of sight
and the skin on the thumb
drawn against it
shudders. I wind up
again, then roll
it to him.
He balances it
like a spear
between us carefully
aligning the air.
He's laughing.
A line sings

through my head. A line
goes through my hand.
Giggling,
he winds up again
but does not throw.
The line will go anywhere
he wants, this
is better than throwing.

With Father, Cleaning Out the Spring

Our legs gulped up in slippery
hip boots, we waddle to the woods.
Mosquitoes nag our ears
as we straddle the spring and dig
our buckets in, pitch bale
after bale of brown water into the trees.
We work fast, swipe hard
to outstrip the spring's recovery.
The water goggles as we chip its face.
Inch by inch the spring's glistening
wet throat appears
until our buckets snag on the sides,
unswallow into the sink,
it's time to climb down in.

I sit, submit both fat rubber feet
to the cold clutch,
let it take the blood pressure of my legs,
swallow me part by part
as a blacksnake swallows a mouse.
My toes strain to contact
the planet I'm supposed to hit
beneath this woozy cumulus. A chill
shinnies up my boots, squeezes
my thighs, nibbles
my groin, numbs my balls
and tiptoes up my belly.
Then my toes bump and my heels
settle, I'm rooted in muck,
staring at Father's silly rubber feet.

I jam the bucket in.
It gags, chokes. I heave it

up. Father lifts it, flings
it at the trees and hands it
back for me to gouge into the slop.
I let it slump, sink,
then wrestle it up against
the suck till it uncorks
with a slurp, heft it
into Father's ready grip.
He lugs the ripe gunk off
and dumps it, splop upon splop,
then rushes the bucket back,
light, ringingly empty.
I sink it plump
into the spring's stomach.

The muck's a warm ointment now.
It's loosening us up.
Father grins at me like a troll.
He's been tattooed,
spackled with fat warts of mud.
I grin back, I'm in
my element. Together
we creak along like an old pump
until I have to bend to dash
the bucket in ankle deep and hand
it up half full past severed roots
and rivulets, past the walls
of the earth's pumped stomach.
And I'm racing the pure water
that streams in like fair weather
thinning the end of the storm,
my bucket scrapes on clean stones,
brings up spoonfuls of pure water,
the spring is clear.

Births

My parents must have kept the cat
for us—our education, a live
experiment. *Chippy*, true to her name,
would regularly retire
to the wicker laundry basket
we'd lug up from the cellar,
where, on stained baby blankets,
while we all closed in to watch,
her body would obey its orders, produce
more glistening raw life
while we encouraged her, stroking,
Nice Chippy, longing to communicate
yet shy, because in each emergency
the cat knew more than we
did or ever wanted to, she seemed to be
listening, and as one came
would speak—not a *meow* but a word,
we were sure, meant something.
Then, with her solicitous tongue,
she'd complete the kitten.

I remember, myself, in the shiny,
tile delivery room, unable
to help my wife—
the clarity of her loneliness.
There's privacy in pain.
The degradation is too intimate,
it must remain a secret.
And that company we press on the suffering
isn't for them. Even mother,
who regrets that in the roar
of nitrous oxide she forgets

our births, who'd explain to us
that perhaps Chippy was afraid—
that a cat can't understand
what's happening to it—could remind us
in her next breath that all except one
kitten must be "put to sleep"
with chloroform—a word which,
I was certain, meant a sweet drifting
off to dream as my parents
tucked the kittens in, kissed them
goodnight.

For a week, Chippy would prowl
the house, a walking minuend, meowing.
Then, as mother predicted, would forget.
I wondered where they went until
among some wood scraps in a cellar
corner I lifted the lid of a rusty pot
to stare at three of them in bed,
clumped cold, their puny countenances
squinched shut. The sweet
faraway hint of chloroform
I soon forgot
until one afternoon, my parents gone,
with a kitchen chair I reached
the bottle. Strange as sex, it was
stronger than a smell, it was a force
that made my heart reverberate,
arranging, grimly tightening
the room, taking
charge of my breath, more serious
than anything I'd meant, worse
than an experiment.

How to Throw Apples

Choose a rotting orchard
where crab apples clot
the grass. The whole
stale afternoon should
smell like beer. Be
careful where you place
your feet; yellow jackets'
feelers move in those
rust-colored dumps
of apple meat. Half
an apple could turn out
to be a live ember
in your hand. Pick
the hard, unblemished ones
whose stems stick up
between their cheeks; they're
worth it. If you get
a green stick with spring
in it and whittle it
to a taper, blunt enough
to make each apple's skin
pucker with a crackle, foam
as you force it in, you can
really ride them. One
whip of that stick and
wow: you can touch
MacKenzies' chimney without
trying—ricochet—
or take the shortcut
home over the trees.

Glass

I used to curve flat stones
at telephone wires to touch
the sparrows off. Grazed,
the green wires twinged. A ricochet.
With Dawson's Daisy pump we'd plink
BB's off those glass beehives
on the poles where the T is crossed.
We nicked one once, but we were never
caught, and nobody's phone went off.

Sometimes on weekends we'd coast
into the swamp, bank our bikes up
the packed muck trail to the New Vernon
Dump, sneaking our tires past
the little sign that said KEEP OUT,
in single file feel our way along
a rut, breaking the peace of chocolate
puddles, back-pedaling to take
the bumps, our gears shrilling
ratchets in the stillness, then swim
into the glare, a sour room
without a roof abandoned in the weeds,
a slum unoccupied for years,
wine jugs left where they
were dropped by busted chairs.

A refrigerator foundered in the wreckage.
I'd splay the first whiskey bottle
off its pate. Gallon jugs bellowed
as they burst. We picked up speed,
any intact glass as quick as
you can grab a neck and winged it

straight into the gale to keep it
glittering, to start the landslide
slithering, make those tin cans leap
with open mouths, because the world is
coming to an end—until the bitter
essence of that dump was so mingled
with our sweat that to blaze more glass
into the mangle wouldn't make any
difference anymore. We were spent.

There was only the quiver of the flies,
the heat. The dump looked just the way
it had before; we hadn't made a dent.
Even then it was too late.
The flies hummed. The air hung sick
with heat. Nothing stirred. Nothing
acted as though it even heard.
And we were satisfied.

To a Boyhood Friend: How We Changed

I know now where
it starts. In Ortman's
garage, with the ancient
smell of gasoline, you
on your back, pinned
down by your buggy,
your hands out of sight
reading braille patiently
unbolting something
I can't see.
I am standing next
to the jack, in the bad
light, as in the entrance
to a mine, the only
person there who is not
working. Somewhere
a greasegun sneezes.
One after another, cars
phone in, sending Roscoe
out the door to crank
the pump and make it
sing like water
running.

I stand there, useless,
my hands still clean,
trying to piece together
from your grunts
how long it will be
before the buggy's ready
to drive back to that rink
we wore in Remsens' field.

I am not thinking
about machines. I am
imagining how the wind
will blabber at our teeth
as we chain-saw dirt
around one end, burst
back into the loud
blue haze we'll leave
over the buzzing
straightaway before
we come sliding into
home again, spewing
the dirt and be
off, making the woods
jittery downhill.

Jimmy, twenty years
it's taken me to say this.
Hanging out in Ortman's
was so dull it was like
pain, I remember almost
nothing. What I picked
up about machines was
this: how shy the thin
muscle of the light
might be along
the silvery forearm
of a wrench,
the delicate hinge
in the wrists of ratchets,
their exact tick,
how Roscoe's swollen hands
could get the leverage
to wedge around and
loosen blocks I could

no more budge than
two hundred pounds
of frozen sod,
the cold chaste way
the sun might touch
the edges of the clouds
outside. The rest
was useless.

Cleaning the Flue

No one else is up here,
and I like it
this way—just me and
my hands, my breath
and my mistakes, just
me and my bête
noire—no more excuses
except to say Here
goes, to wedge, to butt
the unwieldy roofcap
up and lift it
free, letting it loll
like a steel umbrella
beside me while I
peer down the six
galvanized sections
of stovepipe which
I myself zipped up,
stuffed and buttoned
tight with screws,
and see these carbon
whiskers, bituminous
as the hardest
frost, the sparkle
damped out just an arm's
plunge in where
the darkness is
like wool, stifling
my hand which comes back
sullied with the stuff;
to try dangling a broom-
stick in and stirring

around, dinging and
donging the steel's
tang and getting it
back in the face, fleas
of soot swarming
in my hair, the stale
air leaking up
into this polished
afternoon until the nest
is still. The peaks
of the douglas fir
glint, lonely, always
looking off, the sunlight
spare, precise—
the distant eminence
of Forsythe Rock
chiseled out of ice.
I've started something.
It is crouched in there,
a black spider,
hackles up, ready
to explode at the next
fire, and I am happy
now, figuring, warm in
the intent loneliness
of work—just me
and the company of this
problem, intimate,
not talking much,
completing each other's
thoughts. There are no
instructions, so
I bunch a swatch
of polyethylene,
circle it with rope,

cinch it hard, then
bang the ends of warped
rickety one-by-twos
together into a shaky
pole, lug this wobbly
paraphernalia back up,
stuff the crumpled bulk
into the hole, shove
it out of range
and lean on the pole,
drive it further down,
push and pull,
jamming it deeper,
scrubbing the shaft
until the threat is
squashed, and the flue
gives off a grudging
shine, done right.
Finished.

Fixing the Deep-well Jet Pump

Wet guilty parts clinked
in our hands, scored washers,
strange shells with cast-
iron crusts dredged
from the murk and pried
apart, their lining scoured,
ferrous, trout-bright
as the bottom
of a nimble brook
captured and laid open
in the dust.
All day we whittled
decayed gaskets off,
going from one silver
wrench to the next,
each discarded tool a new
coin ringing on cement
as our fingers stumbled
to pronounce the crude
cold vocabulary of flange,
sleeve, bushing, washer, key.
With a dollop of gray
axle grease I buttered
the sealer, forced it
down over the main bearing,
then one by one restrung
the drive shaft
with its deep-sea shells.
The impeller slid into place,
the tightened flanges' mate
as sweet as if I were re-
assembling the day,

joining the skyline
snugly with the sky,
the fit which each rock
made with the air
perfect, no seam where
the outline of any shadow
interlocked the light.
The pump lapped the dribble
I leaked into its throat,
the trickle climbing
step by step from bass
to treble as the pipe
drank. We flipped on the juice.
The jet tensed, the water
firmed, came surging through
the pump, and the evening
was watertight.

Leverage

Right here under the sycamore's masts
is where, when the rest of the family's
asleep and the house becalmed,
I go to invent the wind.
I settle into the slightly seasick swing,
and the night gives a little,
we sink, the rigging rustles overhead.
I pick my feet up, and the anchor's free,
the lawn, the lights in the houses, the whole
state of Missouri set gently adrift.
My pulse begins in the ropes.
I lean back on them like oars.
The sails stir.
A faint breeze comes in from the open sea.
Slowly the prow plunges,
and now the deck is coming back up,
and all the stars are setting at once
through the branches and rising again.
I kick at the stars before they set,
strain on both oars, pull the stars
to me again, the mast creaks,
the earth itself rocks as I row,
I have enough leverage now.

About the Author

Jonathan Holden was born in 1941 in what was then rural New Jersey. After graduating from Oberlin College, he worked in publishing and, later, pursuing one of his avocations, as a secondary school mathematics teacher. He eventually returned to college, earning an M.A. in Creative Writing at San Francisco State and a Ph.D. in English from the University of Colorado. While he was a student at Boulder, his first poetry collection, *Design for a House,* won the 1972 Devins Award.

Since then he has taught at Stephens College, and he is currently Associate Professor of English at Kansas State University, where he teaches Creative Writing and Modern Poetry. In addition to poetry, he has published a critical study of William Stafford, a book of critical essays, *Rhetoric of the Contemporary Lyric* (1980) and has a book forthcoming about the poetry of Richard Hugo.

About the Series

Since 1975, Virginia Commonwealth University has sponsored publication of the winning manuscript in the Annual AWP Award Series in Poetry, an open competition for book-length manuscripts. Established in 1974 in a cooperative arrangement between VCU and the University Press of Virginia, the award carries a $1,000 honorarium and an invitation for the winning author to read at the AWP Annual Meeting.

Manuscripts are received by the series director, who divides them among readers, who are published poets. Finalists are selected and the manuscripts are submitted to a final judge who chooses the winning book. Final judges for the series have included Richard Eberhart, Elizabeth Bishop, Robert Penn Warren, Donald Justice, Maxine Kumin, and William Meredith.

For further information and guidelines for submission write: The Associated Writing Programs, Old Dominion University, Norfolk, Virginia 23508.